More Leads Local

"Empowering Local Businesses for Lifelong Success." Mike Martin

Mike Martin

Mike Martin

Contents

Chapter One

Introduction: Unlocking the Power of Local Lead Generation

In today's hyper-competitive world, generating local leads isn't just a luxury—it's a necessity. Whether you run a cafe, plumbing service, or boutique store, the ability to consistently attract and convert local customers can be the difference between thriving and barely scraping by. Yet, for many business owners, generating those leads can feel like a never-ending battle. You might find yourself spending a fortune on ads, paying for SEO services that yield little return, or struggling to leverage your reputation in a digital-first world.

This book, *More Leads Local*, is designed to change that narrative. It's a practical guide packed with proven strategies to help you generate more leads locally, consistently, and affordably. From search engine optimisation (SEO) and pay-per-click (PPC) advertising to email marketing and community engagement, this book offers a roadmap for success in the local business arena.

But before we dive into these strategies, let me share a personal story—a story of struggle, discovery, and eventual triumph. This isn't just another business theory. What you'll read here is rooted in hard-won experience.

It was Manchester, UK, 2009. I was a full-time locksmith running my own business, and I had big dreams. I wanted to build the best locksmith company in Manchester. I envisioned moving my family into a spacious house, surrounding us with life's comforts, and giving my wife the freedom to be a full-time mother. At first, I thought I was on track. My business ranked number one on Google for "locksmith Manchester," and I assumed the leads would pour in. But some weeks, my phone barely rang.

I couldn't understand it. I was at the top of the search results! Where were the customers? Frustrated, I turned to paid ads. The logic was simple: more visibility, more leads. However, locksmithing is a cutthroat business. Everyone wanted to be at the top of Google. Clicks cost me £10, £15, sometimes even £20, but with jobs starting at only £50 to £100, the math didn't add up—especially when competitors were likely clicking on my ads just to drain my budget.

Desperate, I hired SEO agencies, spending upwards of £2,500 a month. They delivered results—I stayed on the first page—but the return on investment was dismal. I'd need 25 jobs a month just to cover the SEO fees. Some months, I barely broke even. It became clear that simply ranking high wasn't enough to guarantee a steady flow of leads.

I was close to throwing in the towel. The dream I had of building a thriving business felt increasingly out of reach.

The Turning Point

Then, in a last-ditch effort, I decided to take matters into my own hands. I took six weeks off, dedicated myself to learning SEO, and fired my SEO companies and web designers. I built my own HTML websites and optimised them. Slowly but surely, I began to see progress. At one point, I managed to secure the top three spots on Google for "locksmith Manchester." It was a proud achievement—but the results were still inconsistent. Some days my phone didn't ring at all.

I almost gave up entirely, but then I stumbled upon an idea that changed everything.

While researching competitors, I discovered a website called *Manchester Locksmith Pro*. Unlike typical single-location sites, this one had created SEO-optimised pages for every single town and village in Greater Manchester. Intrigued, I contacted the site's owner and negotiated a deal. For a monthly fee, he would redirect all the calls from his site to my phone.

The results were immediate and extraordinary. As soon as the calls were redirected, my phone didn't stop ringing. Lead after lead poured in from all over Greater Manchester. That's when I had my lightbulb moment: it wasn't enough to rank highly for just one major city. The real power lay in dominating every local area within my service radius.

I quickly replicated the strategy, creating my own location-specific pages for every town, village, and suburb I could think of. Within weeks, the number of leads exploded. I went from struggling to secure a few jobs a week to running one of the most successful locksmith businesses in the region. For the first time, I was ahead of the competition, and my business dreams were back on track.

This approach not only saved my business but set the foundation for a new way of thinking about local marketing. As my business grew, I developed a software tool called *Magic Page Plug-in* to automate the process of creating location-specific pages. What used to take me weeks could now be done in minutes. This tool became the backbone of my strategy and allowed me to scale rapidly.

The results were transformative. I built one of the largest independently owned locksmith companies in the UK. The business thrived, my family moved into that dream home, and my wife became a full-time mum as we'd always hoped.

But success isn't a destination; it's a journey. Over time, my dreams evolved. I realised the principles I'd discovered could help not just locksmiths, but any local business. Whether you run a beauty salon, a plumbing service, or a restaurant, the strategies I'll share in this book can work for you too.

Here's the truth: simply being visible in one location isn't enough. Relying on a single strategy, whether it's SEO, PPC, or social media, is also not enough. To truly thrive, you need a comprehensive approach that combines the best of all worlds. This book will show you how to do exactly that.

You'll learn:

- How to dominate local search with SEO.

- The secrets to running profitable PPC campaigns.

- How to use *Magic Page Plug-in* to scale your local presence quickly.

- Effective email marketing techniques to nurture leads and drive repeat business.

- Ways to build and leverage community connections for offline and hybrid marketing success.

Whether you're just starting out or looking to scale an existing business, this book will give you the tools and confidence to take your business to the next level.

What You'll Gain

More Leads Local isn't just about helping you achieve your first business goal. It's about laying the foundation for continuous growth. You'll not only learn how to generate more leads but how to build a sustainable system that supports your long-term success.

So, let's get started. Your journey to more leads, more customers, and more success begins here.

Chapter Two

Laying the Foundation

The journey to generating more leads begins with building a strong foundation. Just like a house, your business needs a solid base to support long-term growth and success. This chapter will cover three essential components: understanding your target audience, building a strong local brand, and setting clear goals. These steps will help you position your business as a trusted local leader and create a roadmap for success.

1. Understanding Your Target Audience

Before you can generate leads, you need to know exactly who you're trying to reach. Your target audience isn't just "everyone in the local area"; it's a specific group of people who are most likely to benefit from your products or services. Understanding their needs, preferences, and behaviours will allow you to tailor your marketing efforts and maximise your impact.

Identifying Your Ideal Local Customer

Start by asking yourself:

- **Who are my best customers?**

- **What problems do they need solving?**

- **Why do they choose my business over competitors?**

For example, if you run a plumbing service, your ideal customers might be homeowners aged 30-55, living within a 20-mile radius, and dealing with urgent repair issues. The more specific you are, the better you can target them.

Tools and Techniques for Market Research

Once you have a rough idea of your target audience, it's time to dig deeper. Here are some tools and techniques:

- **Customer Surveys**: Ask your existing customers about their experiences, needs, and what they value most.

- **Google Analytics**: Use data from your website to understand who is visiting, where they're located, and what services they're interested in.

- **Social Media Insights**: Platforms like Facebook and Instagram offer demographic data and insights into the interests of your followers.

- **Competitor Analysis**: Look at who your competitors are targeting. Tools like SEMrush or Ahrefs can help you see what keywords they rank for and who is engaging with their content.

By leveraging these tools, you'll gain a clearer picture of your ideal customer and how to reach them.

2. Building a Strong Local Brand

Your brand is more than just your logo or company name; it's the impression you leave on your customers. A strong local brand not only makes your business memorable but also builds trust and loyalty within your community.

Establishing Brand Identity and Messaging

Your brand identity should reflect who you are as a business and what you stand for. This includes:

- **Visual Elements**: Your logo, colours, and typography.

- **Tone of Voice**: Are you professional, friendly, or playful? Your communication style should resonate with your audience.

- **Core Values**: What principles guide your

business? For example, reliability, affordability, or exceptional customer service.

Once your identity is clear, develop a brand message that communicates your unique value. Consider this formula:**[Your Business] helps [Your Target Audience] achieve [Their Goal] by providing [Your Unique Selling Point].**

For instance: *"XYZ Plumbing helps local homeowners maintain stress-free homes by providing fast, reliable plumbing services at competitive prices."*

Leveraging Community Involvement for Visibility

People like to support businesses that are active and engaged in their community. Here are a few ways to boost your visibility:

- **Sponsor Local Events**: Sponsor charity runs, school fundraisers, or local festivals. Your name will be associated with good causes and seen by many.

- **Join Local Business Groups**: Participate in your Chamber of Commerce or local business networks to build relationships and spread your brand.

- **Collaborate with Other Businesses**: Partner with complementary businesses to cross-promote services. For example, a café could collaborate with a local bakery for joint promotions.

The more your community sees you contributing, the more they'll trust and remember your brand.

3. Setting Clear Goals

Without clear goals, it's easy to get lost in the day-to-day grind without making real progress. Setting measurable objectives helps you focus your efforts, track your progress, and adjust your strategies as needed.

Lead Generation KPIs for Local Businesses

Key Performance Indicators (KPIs) are the metrics you use to measure success. When it comes to lead generation, some essential KPIs include:

- **Number of Leads**: How many potential customers are reaching out to your business?

- **Lead Conversion Rate**: What percentage of those leads are turning into paying customers?

- **Cost Per Lead (CPL)**: How much are you spending to generate each lead? This includes ad spend, SEO costs, and time investment.

- **Customer Lifetime Value (CLV)**: How much revenue does a customer bring in over the entire relationship with your business?

Tracking these metrics helps you understand what's working and where to make improvements.

Creating Actionable and Measurable Marketing Objectives

Your goals should be **SMART**:

- **Specific**: Clearly define what you want to achieve.

- **Measurable**: Include metrics to track progress.

- **Achievable**: Set goals that are challenging but realistic.

- **Relevant**: Align goals with your overall business objectives.

- **Time-Bound**: Set deadlines to stay on track.

For example:

- *"Increase the number of leads by 25% in the next three months through improved SEO and targeted PPC campaigns."*

- *"Reduce Cost Per Lead by 10% within six months by optimising ad spend and refining targeting. "*

With clear goals in place, you'll have a roadmap to guide your efforts and keep you accountable.

Laying a Strong Foundation for Success

Understanding your target audience, building a strong local brand, and setting clear goals are foundational steps for any local business aiming to generate more leads. These elements will not only help you attract more customers but also ensure your marketing efforts are efficient and effective.

In the next chapter, we'll dive into the world of online strategies, starting with mastering local SEO—a crucial tool for any business that wants to dominate its local market.

Chapter Three

Mastering Online Strategies

The digital world offers an unparalleled opportunity for local businesses to expand their reach and generate more leads. However, it can also be a daunting space to navigate. This chapter will focus on three key online strategies: Search Engine Optimisation (SEO), Pay-Per-Click (PPC) Advertising, and Social Media Marketing. By mastering these tactics, you'll be able to increase your business's visibility, attract more local customers, and boost your bottom line.

1. Search Engine Optimisation (SEO) for Local Visibility

The Importance of Local SEO

For most local businesses, the journey to finding new customers begins with a search engine. Whether someone needs a plumber, hairdresser, or restaurant, they'll often turn to Google to find the best option near them. This is where local SEO comes in.

Local SEO helps your business appear in search results when people search for services in your area. Unlike traditional SEO, which focuses on ranking globally, local SEO is about dominating the local market and ensuring your business appears when and where it matters most.

Optimising Your Google Business Profile

One of the most powerful tools for local SEO is a **Google Business Profile (GBP)**. Optimising your

GBP profile can dramatically improve your local search visibility. Here's how:

- **Complete Your Profile**: Ensure your GBP profile includes accurate business information, such as your name, address, phone number, and hours of operation.

- **Add Photos and Videos**: Showcase your products, services, and premises to build trust and attract more customers.

- **Encourage Reviews**: Positive customer reviews not only boost your credibility but also improve your local ranking.

- **Utilise Posts and Updates**: Share promotions, events, or updates directly on your GBP profile to keep your audience engaged.

Using Local Keywords and Geo-Targeted Content

To rank well in local searches, you need to incorporate local keywords into your website's content. This includes:

- **Location-Specific Keywords**: Use terms like "plumber in Leeds" or "Manchester cafe near me" throughout your site.

- **Geo-Targeted Landing Pages**: Create individual pages targeting specific areas within your service radius. These pages should include tailored content relevant to each location.

- **Schema Markup**: Implement local business schema to help search engines understand your business better and display relevant information in search results.

For a more comprehensive understanding of local SEO, I highly recommend reading *The Complete Local SEO Playbook 2025*. This book provides a step-by-step guide to mastering every aspect of local SEO, from technical optimisation to content strategy.

2. Pay-Per-Click (PPC) Advertising

Introduction to PPC for Local Businesses

While SEO is a long-term strategy, PPC advertising offers immediate visibility. With PPC, you pay to appear at the top of search results or in social media feeds, ensuring your business is seen by potential customers right away.

Google Ads and Geo-Targeted Campaigns

Google Ads is one of the most effective platforms for PPC advertising. With geo-targeted campaigns, you can:

- **Target Specific Locations**: Ensure your ads only appear to users within a defined geographic area, such as a city, town, or even a specific postcode.

- **Bid on Local Keywords**: Invest in keywords

that potential customers are searching for, such as "emergency locksmith London."

- **Use Ad Extensions**: Add extra information to your ads, such as a phone number, location, or direct links to specific pages.

A well-optimised Google Ads campaign can drive highly targeted traffic to your website and generate leads almost immediately.

Using Facebook Ads for Local Engagement

Facebook Ads provide another powerful platform for local PPC campaigns. By leveraging Facebook's detailed targeting options, you can:

- **Reach a Local Audience**: Target users based on their location, age, interests, and even behaviour.

- **Promote Special Offers**: Use Facebook Ads to highlight time-sensitive promotions or discounts.

- **Drive Engagement**: Encourage users to like your page, comment on posts, or share your content with their network.

The key to a successful PPC campaign is consistent monitoring and optimisation. Regularly review your performance data to identify which ads are working and adjust your strategy accordingly.

3. Social Media Marketing for Local Audiences

Choosing the Right Platforms

Not all social media platforms are created equal. To effectively engage with your local audience, focus on the platforms where they are most active. For most local businesses, this includes:

- **Facebook**: Ideal for community engagement and sharing updates.

- **Instagram**: Great for visual businesses like

restaurants, salons, and retail stores.

- **LinkedIn**: Useful for B2B businesses or professional services.

- **Nextdoor**: A hyper-local platform that connects neighbours and promotes local businesses.

Creating Engaging, Community-Focused Content

The key to social media success is creating content that resonates with your local audience. This could include:

- **Behind-the-Scenes Posts**: Show what happens behind the scenes at your business to build a personal connection.

- **Local Stories and Events**: Share news about your community or highlight local events you're involved in.

- **Polls and Questions**: Engage your audience

by asking for their opinions or feedback.

Consistency is crucial. Aim to post regularly and interact with your followers to keep them engaged.

Encouraging User-Generated Content and Reviews

One of the most powerful forms of social proof is user-generated content. Encourage your customers to:

- **Share Photos and Videos**: Ask them to post about their experiences with your business and tag your account.

- **Leave Reviews**: Positive reviews on platforms like Facebook and Google build trust and improve your online reputation.

- **Participate in Competitions**: Run social media contests that encourage users to share your content or tag their friends.

User-generated content not only strengthens your brand but also expands your reach as customers share their experiences with their own networks.

Mastering Online Strategies for Local Success

By mastering local SEO, PPC advertising, and social media marketing, you'll position your business for greater online visibility and increased lead generation. These strategies work together to ensure your business is seen by the right people at the right time, driving consistent growth.

In the next chapter, we'll explore the power of combining online and offline strategies to maximise your local lead generation efforts.

Chapter Four

Offline and Hybrid Strategies

I n the digital age, it's easy to overlook the value of personal connections, but people still prefer to do business with those they know and trust. By engaging with your local community, you can build a strong network of loyal customers and business partners.

Sponsoring Local Events

One of the simplest ways to increase your business's visibility is by sponsoring local events. Whether it's a charity run, school fundraiser, or neighbourhood festival, event sponsorship shows that your business is invested in the community.

Benefits of sponsorship include:

- **Brand Exposure**: Your business name and logo will be prominently displayed on event materials.

- **Positive Associations**: Supporting local causes enhances your brand's reputation.

- **Networking Opportunities**: Events allow you to connect with potential customers and other business owners.

To get started, look for events that align with your brand values and target audience. Reach out to organisers to discuss sponsorship packages, which might include booth space, banner displays, or mentions in promotional materials.

Partnering with Other Local Businesses

Collaborating with complementary businesses can help you reach new audiences and create mutually beneficial relationships. For example:

- A local bakery and coffee shop could cross-promote each other's products.

- A gym could partner with a health food store to offer exclusive discounts for members.

These partnerships can take various forms, such as joint promotions, bundled services, or co-hosted events.

Hosting Your Own Workshops or Seminars

Position your business as a local authority by sharing your expertise through workshops or seminars. For instance:

- A gardening store could host a "Seasonal Plant Care" workshop.

- A financial advisor could run a "Saving for Your Future" seminar.

These events not only attract potential customers but also establish your credibility and build lasting relationships. Promote your events through local newspapers, social media, and your email list to ensure maximum attendance.

2. Traditional Advertising with a Modern Twist

Traditional advertising methods like flyers, direct mail, and radio are still effective, but they need to be used strategically and integrated with your digital efforts.

Using Flyers, Direct Mail, and Local Radio Effectively

Traditional ads can help you reach audiences who may not be active online. Here's how to modernise these methods for better results:

- **Flyers**: Focus on clear, compelling design and include a strong call-to-action (CTA). For example, "Bring this flyer for 10% off your next purchase."

- **Direct Mail**: Personalise your mailings based on customer data. Highlight offers tailored to specific neighbourhoods or demographics.

- **Local Radio**: Radio ads remain a powerful way to connect with a broad audience. Choose stations that your target customers are likely to listen to, and craft messages that emphasise your unique value.

Tracking Offline Marketing Through Online Conversions

One of the challenges of traditional advertising is measuring its effectiveness. However, by incorporating digital elements, you can track how your offline campaigns are performing:

- **Unique URLs**: Include a dedicated landing page URL on your flyers or direct mail, such as "www.yourbusiness.com/offer".

- **Custom Promo Codes**: Use codes that are specific to each campaign, allowing you to track where customers heard about your offer.

- **Google Analytics**: Monitor traffic to your unique URLs and track conversions to see which campaigns are driving results.

These tools ensure you get a clear picture of your return on investment (ROI) for offline campaigns.

3. Combining Online and Offline Efforts

To maximise your lead generation, you need to create a seamless experience between your online and offline presence. This hybrid approach ensures customers can easily engage with your business, no matter where they start their journey.

QR Codes and Call Tracking

Modern technology allows you to bridge the gap between physical and digital marketing:

- **QR Codes**: These are a simple way to connect offline materials to your online content. For example, include a QR code on your flyers or business cards that directs customers to your website, a special offer, or a booking page.

- **Call Tracking**: Assign unique phone numbers to different marketing campaigns. This way, you can track which ads or materials are driving phone enquiries and adjust your strategy accordingly.

Both methods provide valuable data to optimise your marketing efforts and improve lead generation.

Bridging the Gap Between Physical Stores and Digital Marketing

If your business has a physical location, it's essential to integrate your in-store experience with your digital efforts:

- **In-Store Promotions**: Encourage customers to follow you on social media or sign up for your email list by offering discounts or exclusive deals.

- **Digital Displays**: Use digital screens in your store to promote online offers, new products, or upcoming events.

- **Customer Feedback**: Use in-store kiosks or tablets to collect customer reviews and feedback, which can then be showcased on your website or social media.

By aligning your online and offline strategies, you'll create a cohesive brand experience that encourages customer loyalty and maximises engagement.

Harnessing the Power of Hybrid Marketing

Offline and hybrid strategies remain a crucial part of any local business's marketing arsenal. By engaging with your community, leveraging traditional advertising with modern tracking tools, and integrating your online and offline efforts, you'll create a comprehensive marketing plan that drives results.

In the next chapter, we'll delve into leveraging customer relationships through email marketing and loyalty programmes to ensure that your new leads become repeat customers.

Chapter Five

Leveraging Customer Relationships

Generating leads is only half the battle. The true measure of a successful local business lies in its ability to retain customers and encourage repeat business. Building lasting relationships not only improves customer loyalty but also turns your customers into powerful advocates for your brand. In this chapter, we'll explore two key strategies: email marketing and customer loyalty programs. These approaches will help you stay connected with your audience, boost retention, and drive referrals.

1. Email Marketing for Retention and Referrals

Email marketing remains one of the most effective ways to nurture relationships with your customers. It allows you to communicate directly, keep your brand top of mind, and drive repeat business at a low cost.

Building a Local Email List

Before you can reap the benefits of email marketing, you need a robust and engaged email list. Here's how to get started:

- **In-Store Sign-Ups**: Encourage customers to join your mailing list at the point of sale. Offer an incentive like a discount or freebie for signing up.

- **Website Opt-Ins**: Add a subscription form to your website, preferably with a compelling offer such as a downloadable guide, discount code, or exclusive content.

- **Social Media Promotions**: Run campaigns on platforms like Facebook and Instagram that direct users to a landing page with an email opt-in form.

- **Event Sign-Ups**: Collect emails at local events or workshops by offering something of value, such as a prize draw or special event-only offer.

Remember to always get clear consent and comply with local data protection regulations, such as GDPR in the UK.

Crafting Effective Email Campaigns

Once you have a list, the next step is to engage your audience with thoughtful and relevant content. Effective email campaigns often include:

- **Welcome Emails**: First impressions count. When someone joins your list, send an immediate welcome email that thanks them and provides an overview of what to expect.

- **Regular Updates**: Share updates about your business, new products, or upcoming events.

- **Exclusive Offers**: Reward your subscribers with special discounts or early access to promotions.

- **Personalised Recommendations**: Use data from past purchases or interactions to tailor offers and suggestions.

To ensure your emails resonate:

- Keep your subject lines short and engaging.

- Use a friendly tone that aligns with your brand voice.

- Include clear calls-to-action (CTAs) to encourage specific actions, such as visiting your store or leaving a review.

Encouraging Reviews and Referrals Through Email

Email is a powerful tool for building social proof and expanding your customer base. Here's how to leverage it:

- **Request Reviews**: After a purchase or service, send a follow-up email asking for a review. Provide direct links to platforms like Google, Facebook, or Trustpilot.

- **Referral Programs**: Encourage your existing customers to refer friends and family by offering rewards. For instance, "Refer a friend and both of you receive 10% off your next visit."

- **Testimonial Campaigns**: Highlight positive customer feedback in your emails and invite others to share their experiences.

By nurturing these relationships, you'll not only retain your current customers but also gain new ones through referrals.

2. Customer Loyalty Programs

Loyalty programs are a proven way to keep customers coming back. By offering rewards for repeat business, you'll create a sense of appreciation and build long-term loyalty.

Designing Loyalty Rewards for Local Customers

A well-designed loyalty program incentivises customers to choose your business over competitors. Here's how to create one:

- **Point-Based Rewards**: Customers earn points for every purchase, which they can redeem for discounts or free products. For example, a coffee shop might offer a free drink after 10 purchases.

- **Tiered Programs**: Reward your most loyal customers with higher-value perks. For instance, a gym could offer free personal training sessions to members who reach a certain tier.

- **Exclusive Benefits**: Provide members with access to exclusive sales, events, or early access to new products.

Tailor your rewards to what your customers value most. The goal is to make them feel recognised and appreciated.

Using Technology to Enhance Loyalty

Technology can streamline your loyalty program and make it more engaging. Consider these tools:

- **Loyalty Apps**: Many businesses now use apps to manage their programs. Customers can track their points, view rewards, and receive personalised offers directly on their smartphones.

- **Digital Punch Cards**: Replace traditional paper punch cards with digital versions.

Customers can store their punch cards in your app or through third-party platforms like Stocard.

- **Automated Rewards**: Use email or SMS to notify customers when they've earned a reward, encouraging them to return to your business.

Technology not only simplifies the process but also provides valuable data on customer behaviour, helping you tailor your offerings further.

Strengthening Relationships for Long-Term Success

By implementing email marketing and loyalty programs, you can transform one-time customers into loyal advocates for your business. These strategies build trust, foster community, and drive consistent revenue. Remember, it's not just about making a sale—it's about creating a lasting connection.

In the next chapter, we'll focus on measuring the effectiveness of your marketing efforts and making data-driven decisions to optimise your lead generation strategy.

Chapter Six

Measuring and Optimising

E ffective marketing isn't a set-it-and-forget-it endeavour. To ensure you're getting the most out of your efforts, you need to measure performance and make continuous improvements. In this chapter, we'll explore how to track your results, measure ROI, and fine-tune your strategies through ongoing testing and adaptation.

1. Tracking Results and ROI

Tracking the performance of your marketing campaigns is essential for understanding what works, what doesn't, and where to allocate your resources. Without clear data, you're essentially flying blind.

Key Metrics for Local Campaigns

Every business will have unique goals, but there are several key metrics that all local businesses should track:

- **Number of Leads**: How many potential customers have contacted you through various channels?

- **Conversion Rate**: What percentage of leads become paying customers?

- **Cost Per Lead (CPL)**: How much are you spending to acquire each lead? This includes advertising spend, software costs, and time investment.

- **Customer Lifetime Value (CLV)**: How much revenue does an average customer generate over the course of their relationship with your business?

- **Return on Investment (ROI)**: How much profit are you making compared to your marketing spend?

For example, if you spend £500 on a local PPC campaign and it generates £2,000 in revenue, your ROI is 300%. This figure helps you determine which campaigns are worth scaling and which need adjustments.

Tools for Tracking Both Online and Offline Leads

To accurately measure these metrics, you'll need the right tools. Here's a breakdown of some essential tracking methods:

- **Google Analytics**: This free tool provides insights into website traffic, user behaviour, and conversions. Use it to track the performance of your SEO, PPC, and social media efforts.

- **Google My Business Insights**: Monitor how customers find your business, how they interact with your GBP profile, and how many calls or direction requests you receive.

- **Call Tracking Software**: Assign unique phone numbers to different campaigns (flyers, radio ads, online ads) to track which ones are driving calls.

- **Customer Relationship Management (CRM) Systems**: CRMs like HubSpot or Zoho help you track interactions with leads from first contact to final sale.

- **Manual Tracking for Offline Campaigns**: For offline efforts like direct mail or event sponsorships, use promo codes, unique URLs, or simple surveys to gauge effectiveness.

Combining these tools allows you to build a comprehensive picture of your marketing performance across all channels.

2. Continuous Improvement

The most successful businesses don't just rely on their initial strategies—they constantly test, learn, and adapt. By regularly reviewing performance and experimenting with new approaches, you can keep your marketing efforts fresh and effective.

A/B Testing Strategies for Local Campaigns

A/B testing (also known as split testing) is a powerful way to identify what resonates best with your audience. It involves comparing two versions of a marketing element to see which performs better.

Here are some areas to apply A/B testing:

- **Landing Pages**: Test different headlines, images, or CTAs to see which version drives more conversions.

- **Ad Copy**: Experiment with different wording, offers, or even emotional tones to find the most compelling message.

- **Email Campaigns**: Try different subject lines, layouts, or send times to improve open and click-through rates.

For example, if you're running a Facebook ad campaign, you might test two different headlines: "Get 20% Off Your First Visit" vs. "Discover Why We're Manchester's #1 Hair Salon." By tracking the click-through rate and conversions for each, you can determine which message is more effective.

Staying Updated on Marketing Trends

The digital marketing landscape is constantly evolving. To stay competitive, you need to keep up with the latest trends and tools. Here are some ways to stay informed:

- **Follow Industry Blogs and News Sites**: Websites like Moz, HubSpot, and Neil Patel's blog regularly publish insights and updates on SEO, PPC, and other marketing strategies.

- **Join Local Business Groups and Forums**: Networking with other local business owners can provide valuable tips and firsthand experiences.

- **Attend Webinars and Conferences**: Many organisations offer free or low-cost webinars on topics like local SEO, social media marketing, and customer engagement.

- **Experiment with New Tools**: Emerging technologies, such as AI-driven analytics or new social media platforms, can offer innovative ways to optimise your campaigns.

By staying proactive and open to change, you'll ensure that your marketing strategies remain effective and ahead of the competition.

Optimising for Long-Term Success

Measuring and optimising your marketing efforts is an ongoing process. By tracking your results, using the right tools, and continuously testing new ideas, you'll maximise your ROI and keep your business growing. The strategies outlined in this chapter will help you make data-driven decisions and fine-tune your approach to local lead generation.

In the next chapter, we'll explore Magic Page Plugin, then how to bring everything together with a comprehensive action plan, ensuring you have a clear path to sustained success.

Chapter Seven

Magic Page Plugin: A Game-Changing Tool for Local Businesses

This is going to be a short chapter, but it's one of the most important in the entire book. The reason? Magic Page Plugin. This tool was the catalyst that enabled me to grow my tiny locksmith business in Manchester, UK, into one of the largest independently owned locksmith companies in the country. It's not just another tool; it's a business transformation engine.

How It Transformed My Business

Let me give you a bit of context. When I first started my locksmith business, I was just one guy with big dreams. Fast forward a few years, and I had built a company with over **800 subcontractors** operating nationwide. Every day, we fielded hundreds of leads and jobs, managed by a small but efficient team of **10 full-time staff** in the office. These employees handled everything from answering calls to distributing jobs, while the locksmiths on the road—who were all self-employed subcontractors—delivered the services.

The business model was simple but highly profitable. We kept **50% of the profit from every job** the subcontractors completed, which made the company a significant amount of money. Over time, it wasn't about the money anymore. I had achieved my first dream and felt it was time to move on. So, I handed the business over to my brother and sister, who still run it to this day—almost a decade later. It's still standing strong because of the solid foundations I built with the help of Magic Page Plugin.

What Makes Magic Page Plugin So Powerful?

The core of this Plugin's brilliance lies in its ability to **create SEO-optimised pages** for every location within your target area—quickly and easily. Here's how it works:

1. Simplified Content Creation

Most businesses make the mistake of trying to create dozens of location pages manually or covering an overly broad area with generic content. This often looks spammy to Google, which can hurt your rankings.

With Magic Page Plugin, you only need to create **one page of content**. The Plugin dynamically generates unique, SEO-optimised pages for every single area within your chosen radius. For instance, if you're a plumber based in Weymouth, England, you could target every village and suburb within a 3-5 mile radius.

2. Dynamic Updates Across All Pages

One of the Plugin's standout features is its ability to make **dynamic updates**. Let's say you're running a seasonal promotion. You can update the offer on one central page, and the Plugin will instantly push that update to every single location page. This saves hours of manual work and ensures consistency across your site.

3. Dominate Local Search Results

By targeting specific locations, Magic Page Plugin allows you to rank for **100% of search queries** related to your service in your area. Whether someone searches for "locksmith in Stockport" or "emergency plumber near Didsbury," your website will have a tailored page optimised for that query.

Affordable and Accessible for Any Business

Here's another reason I'm including this chapter: Magic Page Plugin is incredibly affordable. Many business tools cost anywhere from £100 to £400 per month. Magic Page Plugin, however, starts at just **$9 .99 per month** for a single website. Even with VAT, it's still a fraction of the cost of other tools, making it accessible for small businesses that need to make every penny count.

If you're managing multiple websites or want to expand your reach even further, there are higher-tier plans available, but the basic plan alone is transformational for most local businesses.

How to Get Started with Magic Page Plugin

Implementing Magic Page Plugin is straightforward:

1. **Install it on your WordPress website.**

2. **Create a single page of content.** This should highlight your services and include key information about your business.

3. **Set your target radius.** The Plugin will then generate unique pages for every location within that radius.

4. **Watch your leads grow.** As the pages start ranking, you'll notice an increase in traffic and leads from all over your target area.

For example, if you're based in Manchester City Centre and want to cover a 4-mile radius, you could easily generate pages for 50 or more locations. Each of those pages would be optimised for local searches, giving you unparalleled reach.

A Must-Have Tool for Struggling Local Businesses

If you're a local business owner struggling to generate leads, Magic Page Plugin can change everything. It's not just another expense; it's an investment that pays for itself many times over by increasing your visibility and driving more leads to your business.

This tool helped me build a business that exceeded my wildest expectations, and I'm confident it can do the same for you. Whether you're just starting or looking to scale your operations, Magic Page Plugin provides a clear path to dominating your local market.

Chapter Eight

Conclusion: Putting It All Together

You've made it to the end of this book, but the journey to growing your local business is just beginning. By now, you've explored a range of powerful strategies designed to help you generate more leads, retain loyal customers, and build a thriving business in your local market. From mastering SEO and PPC to leveraging customer relationships and combining online and offline efforts, you have a comprehensive toolkit at your disposal.

Now it's time to take action.

A Step-by-Step Action Plan for Implementing the Strategies

To help you get started, here's a simple action plan to implement what you've learned:

Step 1: Understand Your Target Audience

Before anything else, define who you're trying to reach. Use the tools and techniques outlined in Chapter 1 to identify your ideal customer, their needs, and where they spend their time.

Step 2: Build a Strong Local Brand

Create a compelling brand identity that resonates with your audience. Ensure your messaging is clear and consistent across all platforms, from your website to social media.

Step 3: Optimise Your Online Presence

- Set up and fully optimise your Google Business profile.

- Use Magic Page Plugin to create SEO-optimised location pages for every area you want to target.

- Invest in PPC campaigns with geo-targeted ads on Google and social media platforms.

Step 4: Leverage Offline and Hybrid Strategies

- Get involved in your community through sponsorships, events, and partnerships.

- Use traditional advertising like flyers and radio ads, but integrate them with digital tools like QR codes and call tracking to measure effectiveness.

Step 5: Build and Nurture Customer Relationships

- Start an email marketing campaign to keep your audience engaged and informed.

- Implement a customer loyalty program to reward repeat business and encourage referrals.

Step 6: Track, Measure, and Adjust

- Regularly review your performance metrics, such as leads generated, conversion rates, and ROI.

- Use A/B testing to refine your strategies and improve results.

Encouragement to Test, Measure, and Adjust

No marketing strategy is perfect from the start. Success in local business marketing requires a willingness to experiment and adapt. Some strategies will work brilliantly; others may need tweaking or even discarding. The key is to remain flexible and data-driven.

Here are a few tips:

- **Test Small, Scale Big**: Start with smaller campaigns to see what works. Once you have a winning formula, scale up your efforts.

- **Embrace Failure as a Learning Opportunity**: Not every tactic will succeed, and that's okay. Use each setback as a chance to refine your approach.

- **Stay Consistent**: Marketing is a marathon, not a sprint. Consistent effort over time will yield the best results.

Final Thoughts on Growing a Local Business Through Smarter Marketing

Growing a successful local business is no small feat, but with the right strategies and mindset, it's absolutely achievable. Remember, the goal isn't just to generate more leads—it's to build a sustainable system that attracts, converts, and retains customers over the long term.

As you implement the techniques in this book, keep your goals in mind and take it one step at a time. Celebrate your wins, learn from your challenges, and never stop looking for ways to improve.

Your business has the potential to become a cornerstone of your community, providing value to customers and creating a legacy you can be proud of. Now, it's up to you to make it happen.

Here's to your success!

Chapter Nine

Appendicies

This section provides additional tools and resources to help you apply the strategies discussed in this book. From further learning materials to ready-to-use templates, the appendices are designed to support your journey in building a thriving local business.

Resources for Further Learning

To deepen your understanding of the topics covered in this book, consider exploring the following resources:

Books and Guides

- *The Complete Local SEO Playbook 2025* – A comprehensive guide to mastering local SEO, covering everything from keyword research to technical optimisation.

- *Building a StoryBrand* by Donald Miller – Learn how to craft clear and compelling brand messages that resonate with your audience.

- *Contagious: How to Build Word of Mouth in the Digital Age* by Jonah Berger – Insights into creating shareable content and boosting word-of-mouth marketing.

Online Tools and Platforms

- **Google Analytics**: Essential for tracking website performance and user behaviour.

- **SEMrush and Ahrefs**: All-in-one tools for SEO, PPC, and competitive analysis.

- **Canva**: A user-friendly graphic design tool to create marketing materials.

Courses and Webinars

- **HubSpot Academy**: Offers free courses on digital marketing, email marketing, and customer engagement.

- **Moz Academy**: A great resource for learning about SEO, both local and general.

- **Google Skillshop**: Free courses to help you master Google Ads and other Google tools.

Templates for Marketing Plans, Email Campaigns, and PPC Setups

To streamline your marketing efforts, use the following templates as a starting point:

1. Marketing Plan Template

Objective: [Define your main goal, e.g., "Increase local leads by 20% in six months."]

Target Audience: [Detail your ideal customer, e.g., "Homeowners aged 30-55 in Manchester."]

Key Strategies:

- Local SEO

- PPC campaigns

- Email marketing
  Budget: [Specify your budget for each strategy.]
  Timeline: [Set deadlines for each phase of implementation.]
  Metrics: [List KPIs to track success, such as leads, conversion rates, and ROI.]

2. Email Campaign Template

Subject Line: [e.g., "Get 10% Off Your Next Service!"]

Greeting: [e.g., "Hi [First Name],"]
Body:

- Introduce your offer or update.

- Highlight the benefits of your service.

- Include a strong call-to-action (CTA), such as "Book Now" or "Learn More."
  Closing: [e.g., "Thank you for choosing [Your Business Name]."]
  CTA Button: [e.g., "Claim Your Discount" linking to your landing page.]

3. PPC Campaign Setup Checklist

- **Define Campaign Goal**: [e.g., Drive traffic, generate leads.]

- **Set Target Audience**: [Location, age, interests, etc.]

- **Choose Keywords**: Use tools like Google Keyword Planner to select high-performing local keywords.

- **Create Ad Copy**: Write engaging headlines and descriptions with clear CTAs.

- **Set Budget**: Allocate daily or monthly spend limits.

- **Launch and Monitor**: Track performance and adjust bids or targeting as needed.

Glossary of Key Marketing Terms

Here's a quick reference guide to some of the marketing terms used throughout this book:

- **A/B Testing**: A method of comparing two versions of a marketing element (e.g., ad copy or landing pages) to see which performs better.

- **Call-to-Action (CTA)**: A prompt encouraging the audience to take a specific action, such as "Sign Up" or "Buy Now."

- **Cost Per Lead (CPL)**: The cost of generating a single lead through marketing efforts.

- **Customer Lifetime Value (CLV)**: The total revenue a business expects from a customer over the course of their relationship.

- **Geo-Targeting**: Customising content or ads based on a user's geographic location.

- **Key Performance Indicators (KPIs)**: Metrics used to evaluate the success of a campaign.

- **Pay-Per-Click (PPC)**: A digital advertising model where businesses pay each time a user clicks on their ad.

- **Search Engine Optimisation (SEO)**: The process of improving a website's visibility in organic search results.

- **Target Audience**: A specific group of people most likely to benefit from your product or service.

Acknowledgments

This book wouldn't have been possible without the support and inspiration of so many people.

First, I'd like to thank my family for their unwavering encouragement and understanding throughout this journey. To my brother and sister, who continue to run the locksmith business I built, thank you for keeping the legacy alive and showing me that hard work and dedication truly pay off.

I'm deeply grateful to the incredible community of business owners I've worked with over the years. Your stories, struggles, and successes have been a constant source of motivation and learning.

A special thanks to the creators of Magic Page Plugin for developing such a transformational tool, and to the countless clients and colleagues who've shared their insights and feedback. Your input has been invaluable in shaping the strategies outlined in this book.

Finally, to you, the reader: thank you for taking the time to invest in your business's future. I hope the tools, techniques, and stories in this book inspire you to take bold steps toward achieving your goals. Here's to your success!

Chapter Ten

More by Mike Martin

As we reach the conclusion of this book, it's the perfect time to introduce you to more resources that will expand your understanding of marketing, sales, and entrepreneurship. Each of my books is designed to provide clear, actionable insights that you can apply immediately. Let's take a brief look at each one:

In A World Full of Sheep, Fuck You I'm an Entrepreneur *(the best book I ever wrote)*

For those who dare to break the mould and forge their own path, this book is a manifesto for entrepreneurial rebellion. It's about rejecting conformity, embracing individuality, and pushing boundaries in business and life. I share personal stories, practical advice, and the mindset shifts needed to thrive in a world that often values the status quo. This book is for the true mavericks who are ready to say, "I'm an entrepreneur, and I'm unapologetically proud of it."

The Sales Parables

This book uses storytelling to teach valuable lessons in sales. Through engaging stories and real-world examples, I provide insights into clever sales strategies and techniques that stick. It's designed to inspire and educate, showing you how to connect with customers and close deals effectively. If you've ever struggled with sales or want to refine your approach, *The Sales Parables* offers timeless wisdom in an engaging format.

The One Sentence Marketing Course

In this book, I distil everything you need to know about marketing into a single, powerful sentence. It's a no-nonsense guide that breaks down marketing to its core principles, giving you a straightforward formula to apply to any industry or business. If you want to cut through the noise and master marketing with clarity, this book is your go-to guide.

The One Sentence Storytelling Course

This book teaches you the art of storytelling in its simplest form. I break down storytelling into a single sentence structure that you can use to craft compelling narratives for marketing, sales, and communication. Whether you want to captivate an audience, close a deal, or simply engage people better, this book provides you with a practical framework to become a powerful storyteller.

How to Create the Perfect Sales Webinar

Webinars are one of the most powerful tools in digital marketing, and this book shows you exactly how to craft the perfect one. From structuring your message to engaging your audience and closing sales, this book covers every detail you need to know. Whether you're new to webinars or looking to refine your strategy, you'll find all the essential techniques for turning your presentations into high-converting sales machines.

Get Rich with Digital Real Estate

This book explores the lucrative world of digital real estate. Learn how to build and profit from online properties, dominate local markets, and create streams of passive income. It's a practical guide for entrepreneurs looking to leverage digital assets for long-term wealth. If you're interested in building an online empire, this book provides the blueprint to make it happen.

The Complete Local SEO Playbook

This comprehensive resource offers in-depth insights and practical steps to help your business dominate local search results. It's designed to equip you with the knowledge and tools necessary to enhance your online visibility and attract local customers effectively.

Each of these books is crafted to empower you with the skills, knowledge, and mindset needed to excel in business and beyond. If you've found value in this book, you'll undoubtedly discover even more tools and inspiration in these titles. Explore, learn, and take your entrepreneurial journey to the next level with my collection of practical and insightful resources.

I'm also available to speak on these subjects for podcasts, events, and other platforms. To schedule a conversation, simply book a chat with me at mikem artin.uk.

All the best,

Mike Martin

https://mikemartin.uk